THE WAY WE WEAR

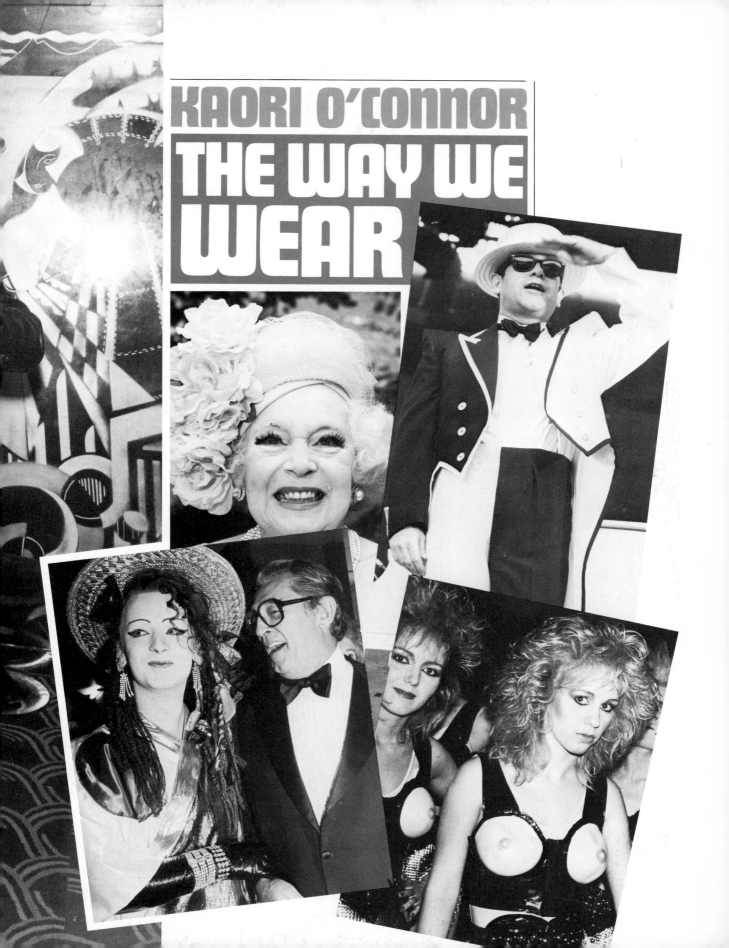

KAORI O'CONNOR
THE WAY WE WEAR

Vermilion & Company Limited

An imprint of the Hutchinson Publishing Group

17–21 Conway Street, London WIP 6JD

Hutchinson Publishing Group (Australia) Pty Ltd
16–22 Church Street, Hawthorn, Melbourne,
Victoria 3122

Hutchinson Group (NZ) Ltd
32–34 View Road, PO Box 40-086, Glenfield,
Auckland 10

Hutchinson Group (SA) Pty Ltd
PO Box 337, Bergvlei 2012, South Africa

First published 1985
© Kaori O'Connor 1985

Set in Linotron Univers Condensed by
Tradespools Limited, Frome, Somerset

Printed in Great Britain by
Butler and Tanner Ltd, Frome and London

Bound in Great Britain by Anchor Brendan Ltd,
Tiptree, Essex

British Library Cataloguing in Publication Data
The Way we wear.
1. Fashion—Pictorial works
I. O'Connor, Kaori
746.9'2   TT506

ISBN 0 09 160141 X

INTRODUCTION

The way we wear says more about us than anything else we do. Like it or not, in today's world we judge and are judged by appearances. And although beauty may only be skin deep, these days it is much more likely than virtue to be its own reward. Looking good used to be a matter of vanity — now it's one of survival, with image as important as any other bankable asset or skill. So it's only natural for us to look as good as we can — but most of us don't.

It's all too easy to say that wearing well requires good looks to start with and lots of money, but it doesn't. The secret of style means making the best of what you're born with, and for that, character and imagination matter more than anything else. Take Reg Dwight, your average, cuddly, balding boy next door — the sort who'd go unnoticed in an empty room. His determination to make himself the centre of attention with the aid of a collection of outrageous clothes, hats and glasses did more for his career than any of his records under the name of Elton John.

Cyndi Lauper spent many years in the back row of backing groups until she stole centre stage in a series of startling outfits that make her look like she's wearing the entire stock of a charity thrift shop. Cyndi Lauper wasn't born rich and beautiful, but she was smart enough to realize that the world is full of talented people. The ones who succeed aren't necessarily the best, but they're definitely the ones who get themselves noticed.

Of course, getting noticed is only the beginning. Once the world knows you exist, there's a right and wrong way of attracting attention. Getting to the top isn't as hard as staying there once you've arrived. And staying there means getting yourself noticed the right way. It was a lot easier to do when fashion was full of rules for every season of the year, and every hour of the day and night. Today, there's only one rule — don't make yourself look ridiculous — and that's the hardest rule of all.

These days there are more ways than ever before to wear well — clothes to make you look taller or thinner, hairstyles to take years off your age, make-up that can perform miracles, and clever accessories galore. But none of them works unless you begin by being objective about yourself and your looks. Cropped pants and high-cut swimsuits look great on fashion models — and awful on anyone who hasn't got the legs and height to carry them off. Just because something is in fashion doesn't mean *you'll* look good in it. The art of wearing well lies in *knowing yourself*, then dressing to maximize your good points and minimize your bad ones. Since it's difficult to be objective about yourself, the best way of learning how to wear well is to watch the people we watch all the time. Stargazing can do more for you than reading a horoscope.

Take Christina Onassis, the billionairess whose doll clothes were made by Dior. When she grew up, her wardrobe cost her a fortune — but she found that spending a lot on your looks doesn't always pay off. Although she could afford the best designers and health spas, her figure problems got bigger and bigger until she fell in love. Once her heart was in it, she slimmed down, shaped up, and would have looked radiant in a flour sack had she chosen to wear one to her wedding. Money is no guarantee of wearing well — what really matters is motivation, and the only person who can do that is *you.*

Strong motivation is the basis of all great diets, and the results of saying no to yourself can certainly be worth the effort, as the dramatic transformations of Elizabeth Taylor and Dolly Parton shows. But just being thin is no guarantee of wearing well — would you like to look like Judy Mazel, the pineapple diet queen? Even having a great face and figure isn't enough — Jane Fonda has both, but the last thing she does when she gets out of her leotards is wear well. Fat or thin, tall or small, fit or not, what really matters is the way you put yourself together.

Wearing well means not dressing in parts — you have to think of the total look. A few elementary principles can upgrade your image completely — or sink it without trace. The wrong stripes can tie you in knots, the wrong belt can cut you in half; some clothes look awful on everyone, others only look good on certain figure types. And however much a certain hair or make-up style may have suited you in the past, if you don't update your image, you'll end up being as interesting as yesterday's paper — unless, like Barbara Cartland, you can go on for so long without changing that you become twice as interesting as today's news.

There's more to wearing well than meets the eye — was it only coincidental that the careers of Farrah Fawcett and Debbie Harry took a sharp turn for the worse when they changed their hairstyles? Is Michael Jackson's voice as good as his face? And why do child stars pay such a high price for early fame?

Wearing well isn't just for an hour or a day — some people, like Joan Collins and Margaret Thatcher, look better as they get older. Others, like Queen Elizabeth the Queen Mother, develop a personal style that becomes an international institution. It's never too late to learn how to do it, and whoever you are, however you live, wearing well is the best revenge

WHAT DO WE WEAR...

NOT A LOT · Tell-all model **Vicki Hodge** being cheeky

NOT ENOUGH · **Susan Anton** braless in a flattening see-through dress — a flesh-coloured bra would have been better

...UNDER WHAT WE WEAR?

NOT FOR LONG · **Anthony Delon**, son of actor Alain Delon, well on the way to baring all

NOT BAD · The **Hot Gossip** girls wearing vests tucked underneath their breasts

OFF THE SHOULDER

THE BIG SQUEEZE · A strapless dress can be breathtaking — but not if you happen to be wearing it, because tightness is all that keeps it up. Worst of all, when a dress like this gets you in its clutches, it pushes your back round to the front, or flattens your front and shoves it round to the back ● **Victoria Principal** (below) wearing herself back to front ● **Linda Gray** (bottom) wearing herself front to back

THAT SINKING FEELING · Many ballgowns are designed to be worn on or off the shoulder, but just because you can doesn't mean you should. Dresses like this look good only when the full skirts are balanced with full sleeves on the shoulders. When you pull the sleeves down, it just looks like the elastic has snapped ● **Patti Reagan** (below) trying to shrug it off **Jane Seymour** (bottom) not quite winning her stripes in a £2000 dress

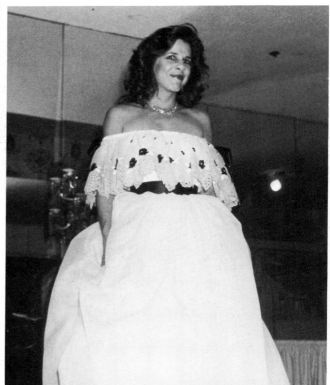

Some unbearable ways to look bare

COLD SHOULDER · The one-shoulder dress has all the problems of strapless dresses and off-the-shoulder dresses, plus the disadvantage of looking as though they ran out of fabric before they could finish your frock

Joan Collins looking tutu much

The Princess of Wales making the best of it

BROOCHING THE SUBJECT

Pin your looks to a brooch-they've been out for so long that they're in

▲ **CLIPPIE · Marilyn** making the most of his cleavage

TAKE A LEAF · from **Jane Seymour's** book – a brooch worn like this can make a simple dress look stunning

DEAD CENTRE · Princess Michael of Kent tries the same trick and gets it wrong. Because the brooch clashes with the rest of her jewellery, it looks like she's sprouted a third eye on her chest

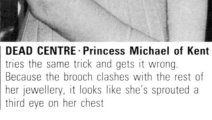

BODICE-RIPPLER · Julie Walters giving herself a shape

TWO-STARR FAMILY · **Ringo Starr** and his wife **Barbara Bach**

LOUNGE LIZARD · **Robert Culp** has a brilliantine idea, but his clip-on bow tie lets him down

PIN-UP · **Michael Jackson** going baroque

WE ARE WHAT WE WEAR...

If you don't have a lot of hair, a great physique or a gorgeous face, and need glasses to see yourself in the mirror — would you have the smarts to do what Reg has done? His glasses are garish, his hats hysterical, his clothes calamitous and his jewellery outrageously joky, but he never goes out in public without turning heads and raising eyebrows, and that's what being a star is all about. OK, so he sings, but so do lots of people. The man is **Reg Dwight** — but what he wears makes him **Elton John**

PRINTS

JEEPERS CREEPERS! Nancy Reagan (right) apparently in the clutches of a killer bamboo plant. A big print is best in small doses. When there's as much as there is here, you don't wear it – it wears you

DUMB BLONDE · Debbie Harry looking like a section of railway siding in a garish graffiti print and matching hat. Gimmicky prints like this attract the wrong kind of attention – people will be more interested in what your clothes say than in what you do

OH MA'AM NO MA'AM · Her Majesty with California governor George Deukmejian, in an outfit that makes her look like a pearly queen. Whoever designed this should be sent to the Tower

NOT WAVING BUT DROWNING · The Duchess of Kent and her collar, struggling to rise above a splashy print. Prints that are too big and bold swallow up everything else you're wearing

Four ways not to rush into print

PRINTS

Prints look best when they're light and delicate, like this one worn by the **Princess of Wales**. It helps to have a bit of solid colour somewhere to add variety, because too much of any print is boring

At best, hats in the same fabric as your dress are too much of a good thing — at worst, they make you look ten years older. If you must wear one, it will look better if you break up the monotony somewhere along the line, as **Queen Noor of Jordan** does with this plain jacket

You get more out of a strong print when you wear less of it. The **Prime Minister's** evening suit would have looked too severe with a plain blouse, but this printed silk is worth its weight in style

Princess Anne shows how to make a little fabric go a long way on a hat. A fabric hatband holds your outfit together without making you look too matched up, and you can make one hat do for several dresses by changing the band

Fit to print

All prints tend to make you look wider, so if you wear them with a plain top or bottom, make sure the print is in the right place. These printed trousers make even **Brooke Shields** look bottom-heavy

Jackie Collins getting the balance right, in a printed top that does great things for her shoulders

Bold print

THE BIG DRESS

Big occasions deserve big dresses – but not too big

THE BIG DRESS · Fashion harpies screeched when the Queen wore this dress by Hardy Amies during her visit to California. 'Too big' and 'too fussy' they said, and as usual they were wrong. Seen in perspective, **Her Majesty** looks regal, dramatic and impressive, while **Nancy Reagan** – wearing just the sort of understated dress that fashion harpies like – fades into insignificance

THE TOO BIG DRESS · **Katie Boyle** (above) in a fancy dress that makes her look like a wedding cake ● **Zsa Zsa Gabor** (right) in a dress that makes her look like a cabbage that's sprouted a head ● **Jane Seymour** in a £6000 ball dress that gives her the figure of an American football player

CHOPPING AND CHANGING

Should you dare to change your hair? Most women are more afraid of going to a new hairdresser than a new dentist, and no wonder. For quick results, the single most effective thing you can do to alter your image is to have a dramatically different new hairstyle. It can change your life — but not always for the best

Sometimes blondes don't have more fun

When she was one of Charlie's Angels, Farrah Fawcett's heavenly blonde curls were the envy of millions. Jealous tongues began to say that her hair, and not Farrah, was the real star of the show. When she left the series she cut off her locks to show her critics that they were wrong. But although she has subsequently appeared on film and stage, her career has never been the same again

As the lead singer in Blondie, Debbie Harry was the first punk sex symbol, an exotic and erotic performer with a voice like broken glass, a face like the young Marilyn Monroe and a wild blonde mane that seemed to lead its own life onstage and off. Like others before her, Debbie found that being a sex symbol could lead to intolerable pressures. In an effort to escape from her image she dyed her hair brown — and her career collapsed. Although she's now gone blonde again, her name is no longer up in lights

Farrah Fawcett long

Farrah Fawcett short

Debbie Harry blonde and dark

From dark to light

Jaclyn Smith, another of Charlie's Angels, was one of the rare brunettes to make it to the top in the blonde-loving world of American modelling. Her dark good looks have kept many of her brown-haired fans from reaching for the peroxide bottle, but she herself is not afraid to experiment with colour. For her film *Always* she looked terrific in a short light wig. Because it's so dramatic, a long mane of dark hair tends to attract attention away from the face but light hair, particularly when it's short, focuses attention on the features. If you contemplate a change as dramatic as this, follow Jaclyn's example and try a wig first

Jaclyn Smith dark and long and light and short

Elizabeth Taylor's change from dark to light solved the problem that many brunettes face when they get older. Most women reach for the dye at the first sign of grey, but dyed dark hair is always harsher than the natural colour, and since most women tend to overcompensate by buying a darker shade than necessary, the result is harsher still. It means having to use heavier make-up to achieve a semblance of balance — but harsh hair and heavy make-up make you look older. That's why wise brunettes of a certain age often opt for going light — light hair and the lighter make-up that goes with it can make you look younger ● **Elizabeth Taylor** dark and light

FAKING IT

It's not true that one piece of real jewellery can do more for your looks than a handful of fakes. Impact is the important thing, and if your jewellery works, it doesn't matter whether it's diamond or diamanté. What *does* matter is the way you think about what you're wearing. It's chic to like your sparklers *because* they're not the real thing. But if you try to pretend that imitations are something more, then *you're* an awful fake

Anna Ford (right) in a witty collar that turns a simple dress into a stunner. If these stones were real, they'd spend all their time locked up in a safe ● **Catherine Oxenburg** (far right) in a diamanté hipbelt that proves that diamonds aren't a girl's best friend

Princess Caroline of Monaco (above) wearing pearls that have never seen the sea. 'I love costume jewellery,' she says, 'it's so much more amusing' ● **Countess Spencer**, stepmother of the Princess of Wales, showing off the 'Althorp Jewels', a collection of sham sparklers sold to visitors to the Spencers' stately home in Northamptonshire. 'Quite honestly,' she says, 'no one can tell the difference'

HANKY PANKY

After twenty-five years of being out, handkerchiefs are back in all the best breast pockets

REAL MEN DON'T USE KLEENEX · Sylvester Stallone with a pocket full of points

Y NOT · Designer **Yves Saint Laurent** with one of his models, in a high-fashion combination of printed silk with stripes

WHY SHOULD MEN HAVE ALL THE FUN?
The Princess of Wales with a hankie that matches the fabric on her hat

EASY DOES IT · Actor **Anthony Andrews**, voted Britain's best-dressed man in 1982; hankies for blazer pockets should be loosely tucked in like this, not folded

NO ONE CAN LOOK GOOD IN FUR

Sophia Loren hibernating in Gstaad

Zsa Zsa Gabor done up like a Yeti

Britt Ekland Thousands of animals are killed on the roads every year, and Britt looks like she's wearing one of them

Fur only looks good on animals, so for goodness' sake, leave it alone

Alana Stewart festooned with dead raccoons

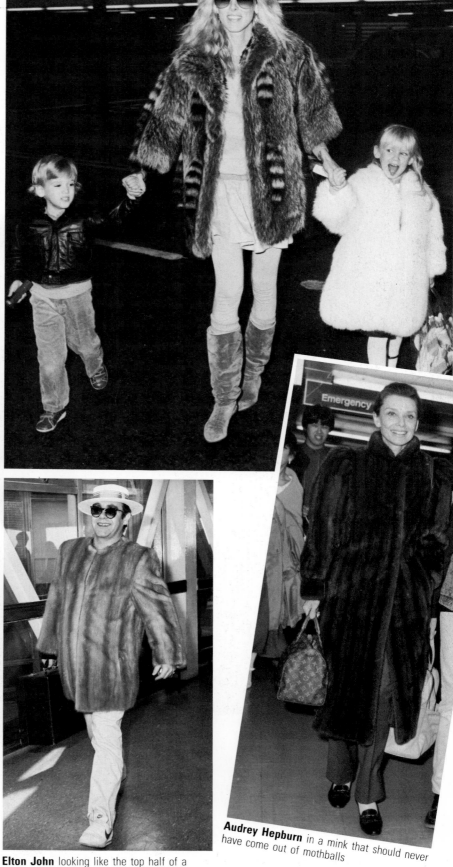

Barbra Streisand in a jacket that makes her look like King Kong

Elton John looking like the top half of a teddy bear

Audrey Hepburn in a mink that should never have come out of mothballs

YOU CAN'T BE TOO THIN – OR CAN YOU?

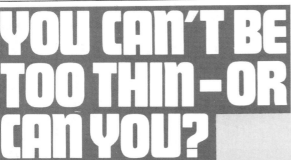

Nancy Reagan (below left) has always believed that looking good starts with looking thin. But with no reserves to fall back on, the strains of public life sometimes pull her down from her usual size 6 to, as she is here, a size 4 – that's a 28-inch chest! Is this really what looking good is all about? ● **Judy Mazel** (below) inventor of the Beverly Hills Diet and the best friend a pineapple ever had, would probably be wearing this slogan across her chest if she still had one. But having followed her own diet, she's barely there. Does it look as though she has enough energy to get off the couch?

No energy problem with jolly Weather Girls **Izora Armstead** and **Martha Armstrong** (above). Who wants to come home to a sour old bag of bones anyway? And doesn't it look like they're having fun? ● **Orson Welles** has always had an enormous talent and a figure to match – now up to 29 stone or 406 lb. So what, if he's big? In this evening suit with its Montparnasse bow no one is going to mistake him for the waiter. Here's proof that you can't be stylish if you spread yourself too thin

DEGENERATION GAP

Tony Curtis, 60, and his friend **Andrea Savio**, 21

Britt Ekland, 42, and her husband **Slim Jim MacDonnell**, 24

Love makes you feel young, but only an old fool believes it makes you look it

GETTING IT OFF YOUR CHEST

BROAD HINT · **Elizabeth Taylor** before she discovered that counting calories is better than counting carats, and a girl's best friend is herself

LABELLED · The only time it's OK to wear a designer label across your front is when no one else can read it. **Olivia Newton-John** wearing a Kansai Yamamoto-designed coat that says KANSAI

PERPLEXING · After increasing the value of John Lennon's estate from £185 million to nearly four times that sum through shrewd investment, is **Yoko Ono** finding it hard to imagine no possessions?

DEFENSIVE · **Koo Stark** saying it about herself before anyone else has the chance to

LITTLE ME · **Princess Michael of Kent** and her stallion, Sprite. Is she really afraid that, despite her efforts, no one knows who she is?

PERISHING · Designer **Katherine Hamnett** meeting the Prime Minister at a Downing Street reception to launch British Fashion Week. No wonder the British fashion industry has so much trouble getting off the ground

DIANA AND CAROLINE
Royal ladies-in-waiting

What did two princesses, both style-setters watched by the world, choose to wear during their time as royal ladies-in-waiting? Their outfits were often surprisingly similar, but always with subtle variations that highlighted the difference between Continental and British fashion. Where the Continental look was chic and simple, the British was soft and feminine. However elegant they may be in other circumstances, there's no doubt that **Caroline's** un-compromisingly tailored Continental clothes were far less flattering to a changing figure than **Diana's** British designs

JACKETS · Buttonless wrap jackets are both comfortable and practical, but Caroline's is too heavy to hang well without being held in by a sash, while Diana's is full and light enough to swing from the shoulders

COATS · Buttoned up like this, Caroline's straight-cut coat doesn't leave her with any breathing space, while Diana's gently flared coat gives her plenty of room to move in and a graceful silhouette besides

EVENING DRESSES · Undeniably elegant, Caroline's dress is more likely to call attention to the hips than Diana's

SUITS · Caroline's boxy wide-shouldered jacket makes her look wide and short when she needs it least, while Diana's threequarter-length coat and matching skirt make her look tall and slim

L FOR LEATHER

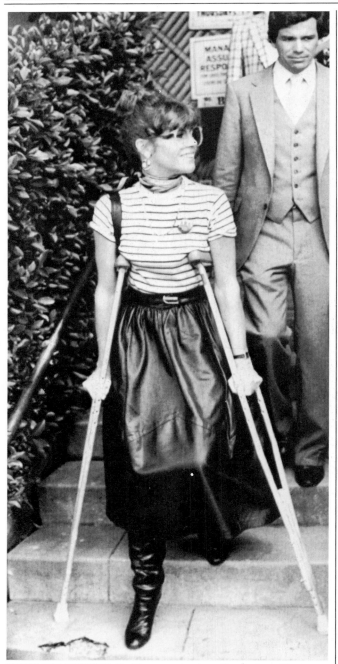

ASKIN FOR TROUBLE · Fashion casualty **Jane Fonda** in a skirt crippled by the wrong shirt. What's the point in working on your body if you cover it up with a combination like this?

ROYAL LEATHER · **The Duchess of Kent** in a graceful pair of trews. Here's how to make leather socially acceptable

Leather suits some like a second skin— but it leaves others on a hiding to nothing

IT'S LEATHER TOO YOUNG TO START · **Rod Stewart** and the Leatherettes, stepson Ashley Hamilton and children Kimberley and Sean

A SKIN FULL · **Joan Collins** giving herself an instant sag. If you're wearing supple leather, hands in the wrong pockets can put fifty years on your chest

SKIN ON SKIN · **Anthony Delon** in leathers from a collection he's designed himself

NO RAW HIDE · **Viscount Althorp** (far left), brother of the Princess of Wales, in a leather jerkin and two T-shirts too many. But armless is better than legless

GROWING UP IS VERY HARD TO DO

25, 30, 35, 40 – when do birthdays stop being fun? Everyone has to face up to growing older – some later, some sooner, and child stars soonest of all. For while people who aren't pretty babies have the compensation of being able to develop their other talents to the full, kiddie twinkles often find that the price of early fame is not having the chance to use the talents they've got if their looks haven't grown up gracefully. Of all the child stars of the great Hollywood era, only Elizabeth Taylor went on to have as successful a career as an adult. It's too early to be certain, but it looks as though not all these child stars who lit up our screens in the seventies will escape unscathed from having so much so soon

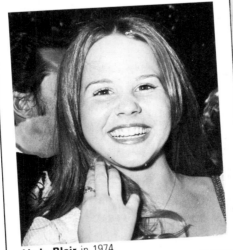

Linda Blair in 1974

LINDA BLAIR · They say there's a jinx on the people who worked on *The Exorcist*, and if there is, baby-faced Linda Blair hasn't escaped it. Her performance as the possessed child Regan has been followed by headlining appearances in court on drug charges, but no more successful acting roles

JODIE FOSTER · Jodie Foster won fame and fans for her performance in films like *Taxi* and *Bugsy Malone*. Sadly, she also attracted the attention of John Hinkley, whose attempted assassination of Ronald Reagan has been linked to his obsessive need to win her love. Although her mother is a top Hollywood agent, Jodie Foster's career now needs a lift badly

Jodie Foster in *Bugsy Malone*, 1977

Linda Blair now ▲

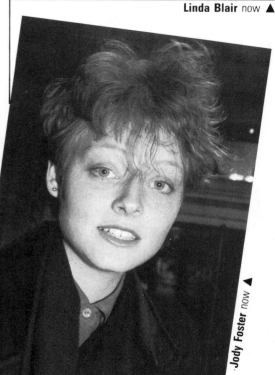

Jody Foster now ▲

TATUM O'NEAL · Hollywood kid Tatum O'Neal's performance as a hayseed orphan in *Paper Moon* knocked father Ryan O'Neal off the screen and won her a special Oscar. But despite a subsequent string of kiddie-pics in the classic tradition – among them a remake of *National Velvet* – her career at the moment is nothing to moon over

BROOKE SHIELDS · Brooke Shields really was a pretty baby, and she already had a successful career as a child model behind her when she hit Hollywood to star in a film that might have been named for her. Today her acting and modelling careers are going brilliantly, and although she has the talent to back up her looks, it's no accident that, of all the child stars of her generation, she is the only one who resembles the young Elizabeth Taylor

Tatum O'Neal now ▲

Brooke Shields now ▼

Tatum O'Neal with her Oscar, 1974.

Brooke Shields in *Pretty Baby*, 1978

MESSING ABOUT

The usually immaculate Nancy Reagan dressed up like this as a joke to raise money for charity. No one else here had a good excuse, and all they raised was a laugh

GOING MY WAY · Alana Stewart in an outfit that seems to be going every way at once. Ghastly though it is, the hitched-up skirt is probably the ideal choice for someone who makes a habit of hitching her wagon to other people's stars

SPOT THE BALL · Koo Stark (left) going for a chic fifties look and missing by a mile. Big buttons don't look right on a bold spot print, and there's no point in having a wide neckline if you clutter it up with a lot of limp hair

RAG BAG · Petula Clark colouring herself scrappy in bits that look like they've come off her dress, her escort and the family pet. Most six-year-olds can do better than this

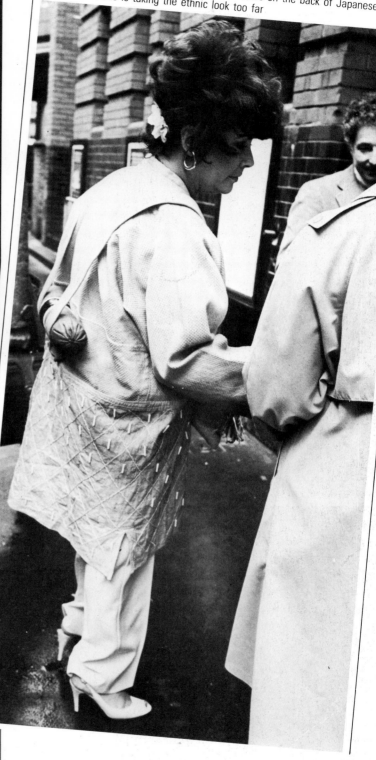

A LOAD OF BALONEY · Elizabeth Taylor wearing her lunch on her back. It's really a roll of padding used to hold up the bows on the back of Japanese kimonos, but this is taking the ethnic look too far

HAS SHE JUST SEEN HERSELF IN A MIRROR? Britt Ekland in a look that's pure sixties – 1860 above the belt, and 1960 below it

YOU CAN'T BE TOO RICH...

Poor Christina Onassis. Dior made her doll clothes, but when she grew up she discovered that money can buy a lot of unhappiness. And since the way you feel has a lot to do with the way you look, she also found out that money can lead to some weighty problems

Christina was always Daddy's girl, especially in looks. Their parents' divorce upset Christina and her older brother Alexander, but Maria Callas — Ari's long-time companion — was never a serious threat to close family ties. Unsure of herself, Christina tried to find happiness in the jet-set circles she was born to. Among her escorts was Thierry Roussel, heir to a chemical fortune, but none of her teenage friendships came to anything more

Teenage friends **Thierry Roussel** and **Christina** (below)

▲ Daddy's girl   Stepmother and stepdaughter — **Jackie** and **Christina** ▼

After many years of bachelorhood, Ari married Jackie Kennedy, and Christina had to compete for her father's affection with the most famous woman in the world. The relationship between stepmother and stepdaughter was never a happy one, and Christina was deeply hurt by what she saw as her father's betrayal

Desperate to escape from a difficult situation, Christina eloped with Joseph Bolker, a real-estate man from California who was 27 years her senior. This time it was Ari's turn to feel betrayed. He stepped in and brought the marriage to a quick end, and Christina returned home in disgrace

...OR CAN YOU?

▼ 1975 Second marriage: **Christina** and **Alexander Andreadis**

In 1973 Christina's brother was killed in a helicopter crash, leaving her as Ari's sole direct heir. It was his hope that Christina would marry into one of the other great Greek shipping families in order to consolidate her position and inheritance. When Aristotle Onassis died in 1975 he left Christina alone in the world with a fortune estimated at £500 million. When the period of mourning was over she married shipping heir Alexander Andreadis. But as marriages made in boardrooms are not the same as those made in heaven, it ended in divorce. In 1978 Christina married Sergei Kausov in Moscow. But by May 1980 this marriage too had ended in divorce

Christina and her big problem

The years of unhappiness began to take their toll. Christina lost interest in her appearance and put on weight. She had all the money in the world to buy treatments, designer clothes and every beauty aid ever invented, but nothing seemed to work. Isolated now by her size as well as her wealth, she became lonelier and larger

In January 1984 Christina checked into another health farm, this time in Marbella, where Thierry Roussel, her friend from teenage days, was also a guest. He promised to marry her if she lost 20 lb, and love succeeded where years of expensive treatments had failed. She lost the weight, and he kept his promise. When they married in May 1984, Christina wore a dress by Dior. Maybe her happy-ever-after is beginning at last

(opposite page) Fourth marriage: **Christina** and **Thierry Roussel**

INSIGHT

Glassy eyes aren't as classy as glasses, so throw your contact lenses away and go back to specs. The way to be in focus today is behind big lenses, the bigger the better, with very thin frames or no frames at all. And don't get caught out by wearing them pushed up on your forehead or tucked into your shirt. If they're not in use, the smart way to wear them is dangling on a chain around your neck

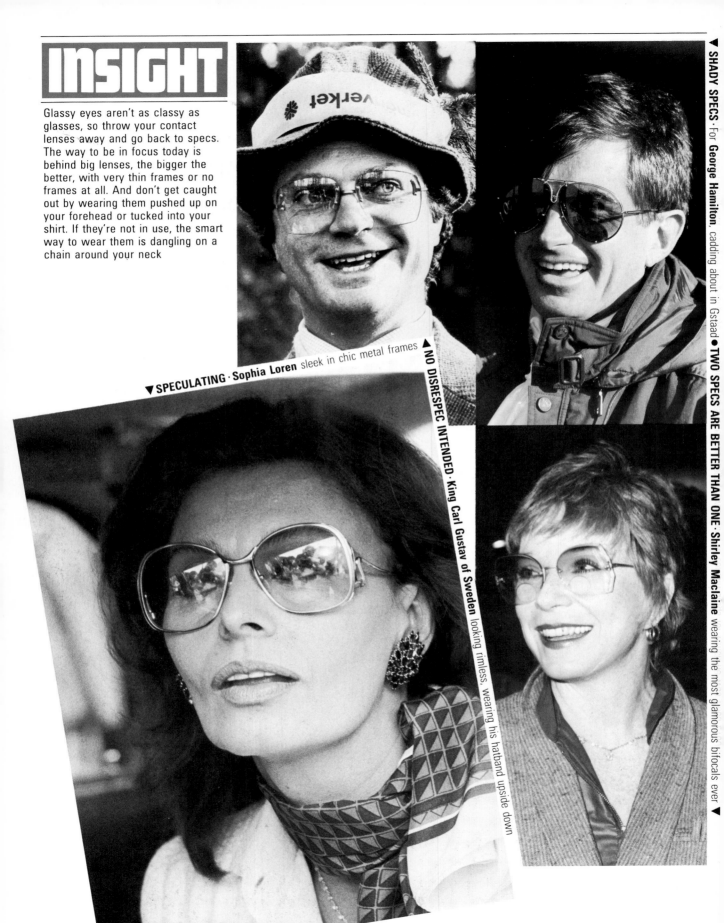

▼ SPECULATING · **Sophia Loren** sleek in chic metal frames ▲

▲ SHADY SPECS · For **George Hamilton**, cadding about in Gstaad ● **TWO SPECS ARE BETTER THAN ONE** · **Shirley Maclaine** wearing the most glamorous bifocals ever ▼

▼ NO DISRESPEC INTENDED · **King Carl Gustav of Sweden** looking rimless, wearing his hatband upside down

▲INSPECTED · **Tony Perkins** finding that being in the public eye had its drawbacks when his luggage was found to contain drugs for which he was fined £100

▲FOUR EYES · **Rod Stewart** and his friend, model **Kelly Emberg** ▼

◄SPECTATING · The Princess of Wales watching polo ● A SIGHT FOR SORE EYES · Actress **Brooke Shields** ▼

BOY OH BOY

Updating your looks is the name of the game if you want to keep in the running. Clinging to the past will make you as interesting as yesterday's papers, and if your hair, clothes, make-up and everything about you are date-stamped 'best before 1979', you can't be surprised if you're left on the shelf. New clothes will keep you in touch with current trends, but it's all too easy to fall into a rut where make-up is concerned. For once you can't spend your way out of trouble, because buying a new eyeshadow or blusher is not going to do the trick if you slap them on in the same old way. Technique is what matters — and no one today makes up better than **Boy George**. He's so good at it that the prestigious Elizabeth Arden cosmetic house in America broke through the sex barrier and put him at the top of a list of trend-setting faces that takes in such all-time greats as Marlene Dietrich and Theda Bara. Arden particularly singled him out for his dramatic eye styling, but the Boy is no slouch when it comes to hair, accessories and clothes. So if you need inspiration before coming to grips with your face, here are some stunning ideas from the best chameleon in the business

BASIC BOY

SCHOOL BOY

BLACK BOY

YOUR BOY

TEA BOY

OH BOY

BLEACH BOY

TAKING THE PLUNGE

GONE TOO FAR · Actress **Annie Ample** all at sea

Barer isn't better, so how low should you go?

GOING TOO FAR · Actress **Edy Williams** at Cannes

FLATTERY WILL GET YOU EVERYWHERE · **Barbra Streisand** with Michel Legrand and Charles Aznavour. Veiled allusions are always more interesting than being up front

PAWNOGRAPHIC·**Katherine Helmond** of *Soap*, in a dress that makes her chest look like two thirds of a pawnshop sign

X MARKS THE SPOT·where this dress should have stopped. Flattened not flattered, **Linda Gray** with Bob Mackie, who designed it

DANGEROUS CURVES·**Zsa Zsa Gabor** (right) almost undone in more ways than one. A spark from her birthday cake has just burned her on the chest

I-SPIED-HER · Pamela Stephenson in a dress that lets you spy much too much

BARELY THERE · Linda Evans in a dress that would have looked just as good on Charlton Heston. Don't show what you haven't got

BRIGHT AS AN UNBUTTON · Angie Dickinson, wise enough to know that what the eye doesn't see, it wants to see more of

TIARA-BOOM-DE-AY

It takes a lot of organization to write up to 24 books a year like romantic novelist and royal stepgrandmother **Barbara Cartland**. And it takes a lot of organization to dress with dramatic impact year after year, as she does. Careful planning is the key to both her books and her looks, and it all boils down to keeping things simple. All her books have happy endings, all her looks are based on the same accessories, and all she has to change is the names and the trimmings. So what if her looks are as similar as the plots of her books? If the formula works, why change it?

1971 · Dark turban hat trimmed with fur, five-strand pearl necklace, large pearl earrings

1980 · Same necklace and earrings, same hat retrimmed with fur

1980 · Same earrings, light turban hat trimmed with netting and flowers, seven-strand pearl necklace

1984 · Same necklace and earrings, same hat retrimmed with veiling and feathers

▲ 1971   ▼ 1980

▲ 1980   ▼ 1984

A TALE OF TWO WEDDINGS

Same groom, same bride, same wedding suit — but what a difference five years have made to their looks. When **Prince Michael of Kent** married **Baroness Marie-Christine von Reibnitz** in a civil ceremony at Vienna Town Hall in June 1978, he was 35 and she was 33, but he looked younger than his age and she looked older than hers

Things had been put to rights by July 1983, when **Prince** and **Princess Michael** went to Westminster Cathedral for the wedding validation ceremony that followed the recognition of their civil wedding by the Pope. Prince Michael's distinguished beard makes him a more authoritative figure and Princess Michael has exchanged her unflattering drawn-back hairstyle for a light upswept style that makes her look younger. Now they really are a perfect match

Vienna, June 1978

Westminster Cathedral, July 1983

BOOGIE OR BOGEY?

Michael Jackson has the Midas touch – his records go straight into gold or platinum, and he's made more than $50 million from the sales of his album *Thriller* alone. His perfectionism and self-discipline are legendary, and it doesn't stop with singing and dancing. Over the last five years the wizard of rock has remodelled his face completely, turning it into a stylized mask that boldly goes where no sex has ever gone before. Only 25, he's already fond of saying 'I'm not getting older, I'm getting better.' But at this rate, what's he going to look like when he's 40?

◀ **1972** · The Jackson Five with baby brother Randy. Michael, 14, is second from the right

▼ **1976** · The Jacksons: Marlon, Tito, Jackie, Michael and Randy

1981 · At 21, with Katherine Hepburn

▲ **1977** · At 17　　　　　　▼ **1979** · At 19

1983 · At 23　　　　　**1984** · At 25

STARS AND STRIPES

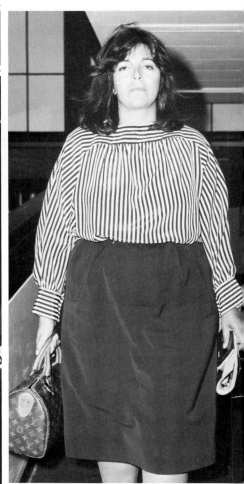

If you wear a lot of stripes, they make it look as though there's a lot of *you*. Overwhelming stripes make even petite **Priscilla Presley** (above left) look huge ● Horizontal stripes have to be straight to look good. The sag in **Bianca Jagger's** dress makes it look even more shapeless than it is

Vertical stripes *don't* make you look thin if you're not. **Christina Onassis** (top right) trying to hide behind her stripes ● Horizontal stripes make you look wide, and you should only wear them if you're as thin as **Nancy Reagan**. But don't wear suits like this, unless you like looking like a xylophone

Dire straights

Only wear stretchy stripes like these if you're as slender and supple as **Twiggy** dancing here with Tommy Tune

Margaux Hemingway, no longer model-slim, is not going to hook any compliments in these overstretched stripes that cling to every bulge

Clingers and clangers

Jacket stripes

Crisp striped jackets make men look younger. **Warren Beatty's** jacket takes as many years off his looks as his friend Diane Keaton puts on with her bag-lady costume

Paul McCartney's stripes make him look even younger – just like a boy who's outgrown his school blazer

Stripes can be suitable away from the city, but only as long as they're light – otherwise you look as though you've wandered out in your pyjamas. Painter **David Hockney** (below), partying with Paloma Picasso, is wearing the perfect tie for his suit – the only thing that looks good with stripes is stripes

Classic stripes like these are a good way of keeping casual clothes from looking too casual. **Viscount Linley** and his sister **Lady Sarah Armstrong-Jones** looking smarter than they're dressed

Stripes along the shoulders make them look broader. **Prince Albert of Monaco** (left), not noted for his physique, serves himself a winning look with this flattering shirt

Vertical stripes at the edge of the shoulders make them look narrow, and if they're narrow to start with it makes them look hunched. **George Harrison** should throw this jacket away

If you wear sporty wide stripes after the sun has gone down, as **Charlene Tilton** of *Dallas*, is doing, it looks like you haven't bothered to dress up for the evening

Wide stripes like **Prince Andrew** is wearing look best on sportswear and casual day clothes

Thin stripes are much more elegant than wide ones. **Barbra Streisand**, who isn't, looks quite long and lean in this evening suit

Even the most refined stripes can do with a bit of stirring up. **Jackie Bisset** turning a simple top into an interesting proposition

Like people, the most interesting stripes are wildly irregular. Bond girl **Barbara Carrera**, dramatic in stripes on stripes

Done up in tiger stripes and matching eye make-up, **Bob Dylan** catches Eric Clapton's eye

Best stripes

You can look great in two-way stripes if, like **Diana Ross** (far left), you keep the lines simple and have a great figure ● Teetering on the edge of looking awful, comedian **Billy Connolly** manages to get away with it by dressing with a sense of humour ● Poor **Jenny Agutter** in a garish combination of three clashing stripes just looks confused

Striping it both ways

Striped tops can make you look taller, and this shirt, worn by **Dudley Moore**, almost succeeds in giving him a lift. But the one dark stripe across his middle pulls him back down to earth

Striped trousers make your legs look longer, and they make them look longest if you wear them with a plain top. **Faye Dunaway** (above) in a subtle stripe that tones with her plain jacket

Going to extremes, **Jamie Lee Curtis** makes herself look even taller and thinner than she is. If she were still going out with Adam, they'd look like the Grasshopper and the Ant ● Regal in Regency stripes, **Princess Anne** makes the most of her height. When the stripes are all the same colour, you can get away with the odd horizontal stripe without cutting yourself in half ● **The Princess of Wales** in a summer version of the leggy look. Striped trousers look best when the stripes aren't too dark and the trousers don't fit too tightly

Queen Noor of Jordan

The kindest stripes of all are diagonal stripes that wrap around the body and make the most of your curves
◀**Liza Minelli** ● **Raquel Welch** ▼

Getting an angle on stripes

La Toya Jackson

SLIMLINE TONICS

You are what you eat-and if you eat too much, what you are is fat. It's what you don't eat that really matters when it comes to looking good

DOLLY PARTON · Physical problems and emotional stress drove Dolly Parton to the shelves of a fridge full of junk food, and she gained 30 lb, over 2 stone, in just 18 months, a staggering surplus for someone who's only five feet tall. Dolly has always refused to reveal her chest measurement, but whatever it was here, it's clear that things had gone too far. After a three-month programme of diet and exercise, Dolly lost the 30 lb and kept her curves in the right places. She also got back the energy and sparkle she lost when her weight was high

The new Dolly (below) with Sylvester Stallone

DEMIS ROUSSOS · Demis Roussos loved his wife's cooking. And he ate so much of it that he put on weight at the rate of 20 lb, or 1½ stone, a year. When clothes became a problem he took to wearing caftans, and ended up by weighing 300 lb, over 21 stone

After deciding that he loved his wife even more than her food, Demis stayed out of the kitchen and went on a strict diet based on chicken. He lost 100 lb, over 7 stone, and threw all his caftans away

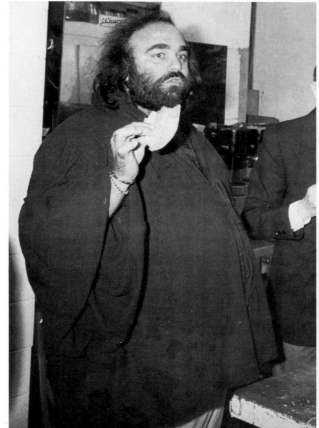

ELIZABETH TAYLOR · Depression, prescription pills and alcohol were Elizabeth Taylor's undoing. Combined with a fondness for rich foods, they bloated her face and figure, affected her health and career, and forced her to hide under tentlike tunics

After a spell at the Betty Ford Center in California, Liz lost 40 lb, almost 3 stone, and was back in a size 8 dress for the first time in years. The new Liz is big news at the box office, and at 52 – with six husbands and 42 years in showbiz behind her – she's never looked better

NOTHING TO JUMP AT ...
Four unsuitable suits

JUMP BEFORE IT'S TOO LATE · Top Hollywood stuntman **Jack Gill** (right) didn't change out of his workclothes before flying to London with his actress wife Morgan Brittany. Was he afraid the plane was going to crash?

NO APOLLO · **Rod Stewart** wearing the crumpled astronaut look

CURTAINS FOR BRITT? **Britt Ekland** with boudoir eyes to match

IN THE BAG · Garment bags are for keeping clothes neat when they're hanging in the wardrobe, but **Elton John** looks like he's wearing one instead. Did he slip into the first thing he saw when he opened his closet door?

COMING A CROPPER

Cropped pants are a hot fashion item – but make sure they really suit you, or you're bound to fall at the first fence

TOO LONG · Barbra Streisand (right) making herself look even shorter than she is. Her jacket, blouse and trousers are much too long for her height. When you get your proportions as wrong as this, it looks like your legs have got lost on their way to your feet

TOO TIGHT · Pamela Stephenson proving that squeezers aren't pleasers. Tight trousers always make you look wider than you are, particularly when they're light. When they're as short as this, they give you thick ankles as well

TOO WIDE · Jenny Agutter (right) shortchanging herself. Trousers like this are cut at an angle from the outside in, and they'll give you a shape – if you give them a leg. By rolling her trousers up, Jenny makes herself look like a blimp floating a foot above the ground

TOO RIGHT · The Princess of Wales wearing the look to perfection. Her cropped trousers are straight and slim but not tight, and end just below the knee. She emphasizes her proportions with a wide belt at the waist, and she doesn't confuse the issue with a jacket

THE QUEEN MOTHER

A smile as an institution

In her early days as Queen Consort of King George VI, the **Queen Mother's** Hartnell crinoline dresses put majesty back on the throne after the trauma of the Abdication, and her exuberant hats and suits in pastel colours cheered the nation through the grey years that followed the Second World War. Her style, of course, is far beyond fashion. But in recent years this is the way we have seen her most often and come to love her the best — in a hat with a turned-back brim, veiled and trimmed for the season of the year; wearing pearls and a brooch but above all the smile, which is the finest crown jewel of the realm

LOOK EAR

How many holes do you wear in your earlobe? Whatever your age and sex, if you're still wearing only two — one in each lobe — you might be in danger of looking out of date. Here's who's wearing how many, now

ONE · Elton John making the most of it. If it's as big as this, everyone's bound to look at the birdie

TWO · Ali McGraw missing the point. Why bother to have two holes if all you're going to stick in them is two little-nothing bits of wire?

TWO · Princess Caroline of Monaco in a winning combination. Neither her hoop nor her star earrings would merit a second glance on their own, but worn together they turn a classic look into something a lot more interesting

THREE · Britt Ekland tripping herself up. Sixties hairstyles and eighties earlobes don't add up to a good look, and the fact that the earrings are identical doesn't help. If you're going to wear three earrings at a time, at least two of them should be different

THREE · Shirley Maclaine tripling up on her studs. If your earrings are simple you can wear three at a time without looking too outrageous, particularly if they match the rest of your jewellery, as they do here. And it's a nice way to make the most of a short haircut

FOUR · Princess Stephanie of Monaco wearing two earrings, with holes for two more

THREE · Cyndi Lauper going for high-volume visibility in earrings so large they cover up her ears. Can she hear herself sing? Does she want to?

FOUR · Mr T in four gold chain earrings to match the forty or so he has around his neck. Only recommended if you have muscles in your earlobes

MUM'S THE WORD

Mothers and daughters

What do these mothers and daughters have in common? Some are lookalikes, some are do-alikes, some are dressalikes — and some don't like each other much. But all these daughters would agree — there's no one quite like Mum

TAHNEE WELCH AND HER MOTHER, ACTRESS RAQUEL WELCH · Sexy starlets weren't supposed to have children in the days when beauty queen Raquel first burst onto the screens in a Stone Age fur bikini, so she had to claim that her daughter Tahnee was her younger sister. No longer a starlet, Raquel has been recognized as a talented actress — and she's kept her looks so well that her daughter now really does look like her sister

◄ **Carrie Fisher** and **Debbie Reynolds**   ▲ **Tahnee W**

ACTRESS CARRIE FISHER, DAUGHTER OF EDDIE FISHER, AND HER MOTHER, ACTRESS AND SINGER DEBBIE REYNOLDS · Pert Debbie Reynolds smiled and sang her way through a string of ingenuous fifties films like *Tammy*, and is still going strong. She recently appeared in the hit play *Woman of the Year* on Broadway. Daughter Carrie's career went straight to the top in record time after her role as Princess Leia in *Star Wars*

CHASTITY BONO, DAUGHTER OF SONNY BONO, AND HER MOTHER, ACTRESS AND SINGER CHER · Chastity Bono became the most famous child in America in the sixties when her proud parents showed her off to the nation on prime time TV during the *Sonny and Cher Show*. Since then, her parents have gone their separate ways, and although Chastity has not yet decided on a career, her mother has been setting a good example, winning acclaim for her first serious acting role in the film *Silkwood*

Chastity Bono and **Cher** ▲

el Welch ▲   **Terri** and **Brooke Shields** ▶

ACTRESS AND MODEL BROOKE SHIELDS, AND HER MOTHER, TERRI SHIELDS · Behind every stage there's a stage mother, and Terri Shields is an unbeatable example of the type. After an early divorce from Frank Shields, Terri threw herself into being a single parent and had Brooke modelling before she was out of the cradle. She scrutinized everything her daughter ate, wore and did from day one, and even today all the work that Brooke undertakes has to meet with Terri's approval. Terri Shields is not an easy woman to work with, and there are those who say that she did not so much raise Brooke as exploit her. But no one can say that she didn't mastermind Brooke's early career with genius. Only one cloud looms on the horizon – it won't be easy when Brooke finally leaves the nest

Nancy and **Patti Reagan** with daughter-in-law **Doria** ▲

ACTRESS PATTI REAGAN AND HER MOTHER, NANCY REAGAN · Patti Reagan has never mastered the high-gloss grooming and immaculate turnout that are second nature to her mother Nancy. Being the President's daughter can't be easy if you want to make it as an actress under your own steam, and having a mother who looks better at 61 than you do at 32 can't help. Nancy knocks spots off Patti and daughter-in-law Doria here, and neither looks as if they are enjoying it. Mothers should set a good example – not show their daughters up

JENNIFER GRANT, DAUGHTER OF CARY GRANT, AND HER MOTHER, ACTRESS AND DIRECTOR DYAN CANNON · Looking more like sisters than mother and daughter, Jennifer Grant and Dyan Cannon enjoy an evening out dancing at the Bus Palladium disco in Paris. It was a double date — both ladies were escorted by their boyfriends. At 17 Jennifer's career is as yet undecided, but her doting father is proud of the fact that she's got brains as well as beauty and has won a place at Stanford, one of America's top universities

ACTRESS AUDREY LANDERS OF *DALLAS* AND HER MOTHER · When the family resemblance is as strong as it is here, mothers and daughters can use the same tricks to look good, and Audrey Landers and her mother certainly do. Both fair, they emphasize their eyes with lashings of mascara rather than with dark eyeshadow, and keep their eyebrows light to heighten the effect. And Mrs Landers has certainly shown her daughter that a fluffy hairstyle can look good when you're older, provided it's not too long

Audrey Landers (right) with her mother (centre) and sister▲ **Jennifer Grant** ▶

Jamie Lee Curtis and **Janet Leigh** ▲

ACTRESS JAMIE LEE CURTIS, DAUGHTER OF TONY CURTIS, AND HER MOTHER, ACTRESS JANET LEIGH · Janet Leigh spent most of the fifties dressed up in medieval costume playing princesses in distress, but she is best remembered for her performance as the murder victim in the shower in Alfred Hitchcock's film *Psycho*. Daughter Jamie Lee earned the title Queen of the Screams after appearances in a string of horror flicks, but is now recognized as an accomplished actress after her outstanding performance in *Trading Places*

SINGER LA TOYA JACKSON, SISTER OF MICHAEL, AND HER MOTHER, KATHERINE JACKSON · Although father Frank has masterminded the Jackson brothers' careers since childhood, La Toya says that her mother's unfailing love and support are the real foundation of the family's success

◀ **Dyan Cannon**　　　　**Katherine** and **La Toya Jackson** ▲

ACTRESS CHARLENE TILTON OF *DALLAS* AND HER MOTHER, CATHERINE · Height, or lack of it, is the one thing this mother and daughter duo have in common as far as appearances go, and neither has really mastered the problem. At a whisker under five feet tall, Charlene Tilton has to be very careful about what she wears, because most things will make her look short or wide. Here she is wearing something that does both at once. Mother and daughter would both have been better off in something plain, with a higher hemline

Charlene Tilton and her mother, **Catherine** ▲

PEARLS OF WISDOM

Forget gold and diamonds — if you want to invest in your looks, do it with pearls. They flatter the face, go well with clothes of all kinds, look good by day or by night, and look better the more you wear them. But if you have a graduated pearl necklace — the kind with large pearls at the front and smaller ones at the side — keep it locked away. Today's pearls are all one size, the bigger the better, and long enough to give you the choice of wearing them low or wrapped around the neck. Here's who's wearing pearls now

ONE ROW · Boy George looking matchless in basic white with pearls

ONE ROW · Lauren Bacall whistling up a smart version of basic black with pearls

TWO ROWS · Zsa Zsa Gabor in a black and white combination that looks great on blondes

THREE ROWS · Jerry Hall (left) holding the biggest pearl of all, daughter Elizabeth

FOUR ROWS · Princess Michael of Kent (right) brightening up a blazer

ENGLISH ROWS · **Joanna Lumley** looking a treat in three strands with tweeds

TOO MANY ROWS · Actress **Sarah Miles** wearing too much of a good thing

ROW IS ME · Actress **Mary Lou Henner** let down by her earrings. The only thing to wear with pearls is more pearls

DIANE KEATON-SUPERMESS

THE ANNIE HALL LOOK · Limp ribbon tied around the neck, worn with or without a wing collar shirt, but always with hair that looks as though it's been dragged through a hedge

Actresses can be more influential than designers when it comes to setting fashion trends, and no one more so than **Diane Keaton**. As Woody Allen's co-star and girlfriend she was given free rein to put together her own wardrobe for their hit films *Annie Hall* and *Sleeper*. On screen it looked like she'd dressed herself from off his closet floor, but her quirky style took off in a big way, and she can claim the credit for having introduced the world to some of the worst looks of recent years

SO WHAT'S NEW? **Diane Keaton** has an on-again off-again affair with **Warren Beatty** and a better-off-than-on new style. Is this how you're going to look next?

THE ROMANCE IS OVER · Diane Keaton has passed her look — and **Woody Allen** — along to **Mia Farrow**

THE SLEEPER LOOK · Shapeless tweed coat, sheepdog fringe and long scarf wrapped around the neck like a boa constrictor

OVER-THE-TOPPING GOOD LOOKS

'Less is more' is one of fashion's favourite rules, but understatement isn't always the best way to get the most out of your looks. Maybe it's because they're musical, but these two stars don't benefit from toning themselves down

UNDERSTATEMENT · Fashion experts would advise **Dolly Parton** to play down her hair and figure by wearing something plain and simple. When she does, *she* looks plain and simple

OVERSTATEMENT · Ruffled blouse, flouncy skirt, lashings of lace and a fussy print – put it all together and she looks great and knows it. What does **Dolly** say to her critics? 'It takes a lot of money to look as cheap as this!'

UNDERSTATEMENT · Fashion experts have been telling **Liberace** to pare himself down to bare essentials for years. But wearing a keyboard scarf and very little else by his usual standards, he looks barely there

OVERSTATEMENT · **Liberace** as his critics love to hate him, struggling to keep his hands up under the weight of his rings. But he wouldn't be wearing so many if his fans didn't love – and pay – to see him looking this way. What does he say to his critics? 'I cry all the way to the bank!'

UNDERSTATEMENT

OVERSTATEMENT

UNDERSTATEMENT

OVERSTATEMENT

BELTING UP

What a waste

Elastic waists on dresses and jumpsuits are meant to make you look shapely, but they just make you look sloppy if your belt comes adrift and shows up the ugly elastic line ● **Shelley Hack** (below) in a belt that's so loose that it looks as though she's lost a lot of weight in the last five seconds

Ginger Rogers dancing down Memory Lane with Fred Astaire, in a dress that makes her look like a sack of potatoes tied up with string

It's a cinch

The easy way to give yourself a shape with a belt is to make sure it's the same colour as the clothes you're wearing — light on light, dark on dark. A high-contrast belt makes you look twice as thick around the middle

THICK · **Diane Keaton** looking like a treetrunk

WRONG · **Andy Williams** cutting himself in half

WHITE ON WHITE · Ali McGraw (above) in a look that couldn't be simpler

DOING IT RIGHT · Barbara Carrera (right) with an extra trick of her own. If you loop your belt over itself instead of tucking it into the belt loops, you'll make your waist look even smaller

It's a cinch

Here's what to do if half of what you're wearing is dark and half light — wear a belt striped in both colours ● **Anthony Andrews** notching up a winning combination

The BIG belt

Big belts can pack a lot of punch — and the bigger they are, the smaller they make you look ● **Linda Evans** (right) in a simple but sexy contoured belt that keeps her from looking like one of the boys ● **Jackie Collins** (far right) hit below the belt by a buckle that looks like a prize from a Golden Gloves contest. Big belts are in — but big buckles are out

Morgan Brittany (above) looking positively studded. Tough belts like this look best when they're backed up with something in leather ● **Joan Collins** (right) with friend Peter Holm, on the way to Zürich to visit her money. You can only carry off a belt as elaborate as this if you keep the rest of your clothes simple.

Double belts

Double belts can look twice as good if you wear them right — and twice as bad if you don't

DOUBLE-CROSSED · Alana Stewart (right) getting it wrong. Double belts don't belong halfway down a full skirt gathered to a waistband, particularly when the shirt is coming out of the top

Belting it out

These two have as much of a way with belts as they do with songs

Cyndi Lauper (below) singing it like she belts, over the top ● **Shirley Bassey** (bottom) belting it like she sings, sweet and low

DOUBLING UP · Royal relative **Catherine Oxenburg**, daughter of Princess Elizabeth of Yugoslavia, getting it right. Double belts look best wrapped around a dress with no waist

HEY SISTER!

Glamorous older sisters can cast a long shadow– but little sisters are full of surprises

Daughters of a top showbiz agent, Joan Collins and her younger sister Jackie grew up in the business and went into acting as a matter of course. Joan went to Hollywood where her career flourished, Jackie followed her there but did not meet with the same success. Jackie gave up acting when she married – but she didn't give up. Instead, she turned to writing sensational low-down-on-the-high-life novels

Joan Collins (below) in 1968

In the seventies, when Joan's career was in the doldrums, a film based on Jackie's bestselling novel *The Bitch* put her back in pictures in a big way and led to her role as Alexis in *Dynasty*. Today Joan's career is going better than ever before, and so is Jackie's. As a superstar author she enjoys more pull in status-conscious Hollywood than most actresses ever get, and her latest bestseller *Hollywood Wives* is being made into a blockbuster American television series that could earn her as much as £14,000,000. Success suits the sisters very well, but while Joan has always been very good at updating her look, Jackie tends to stick to a sixties style. She'd look a lot better if she did like her big sister does

◄**Jackie Collins** in 1968
Flushed with success, **Joan** and **Jackie Collins** now ▼

The Collins sisters

Princess Caroline of Monaco seems never to have gone through an awkward stage where looks are concerned. She had striking features and a strong personality from childhood, was never intimidated by having as glamorous a mother as the late Princess Grace, and obviously couldn't wait to grow up. Younger by seven years, Princess Stephanie was shy, plain and young for her age. At sixteen, dressed by Dior for her first ball, Caroline was a picture of poise and prettiness. But when Stephanie accompanied her father to Henley for the regatta when she was sixteen she was obviously ill at ease, and her turnout lacked the easy chic that was second nature to her sister

Time and tragedy have brought the sisters together. And while Caroline has turned to marriage and motherhood, Stephanie — now a beauty in her own right — is on the covers of all the Continental glossies and is off to study fashion in Paris

▼ **Princess Caroline** at 16
▼▼ **Princess Stephanie** at 16

The Grimaldi sisters

1974 **Stephanie** and **Caroline** with their father Prince Rainier in Austria

Caroline and **Stephanie** now

The Redgrave sisters

Daughters of actor Sir Michael Redgrave and his actress wife Rachel Kempson. Vanessa Redgrave and her younger sister Lynn were born with greasepaint in their blood. Vanessa was the beauty of the family, seemingly made for the limelight, but Lynn had a different look altogether. While Vanessa's flamboyant assurance and classic features made her the perfect choice to play Guinevere in the film of *Camelot*, Lynn stepped straight into the gauche and giggly part she played in the film *Georgie Girl*, and found it difficult to step out afterwards

The comparisons that were always being made between the sisters finally drove Lynn to America. And, strangely for a woman who was always being asked to play queens, Vanessa became more and more involved in the politics of the left-wing Worker's Revolutionary Party and causes it endorsed, to the detriment of her career. Today Lynn has established herself as a successful television actress in America, while Vanessa seems to prefer her political roles to glamorous parts on stage and screen

▲ **Vanessa** now

Lynn now ▼

▲ **Vanessa** in 1967

Lynn in 1967 ▼

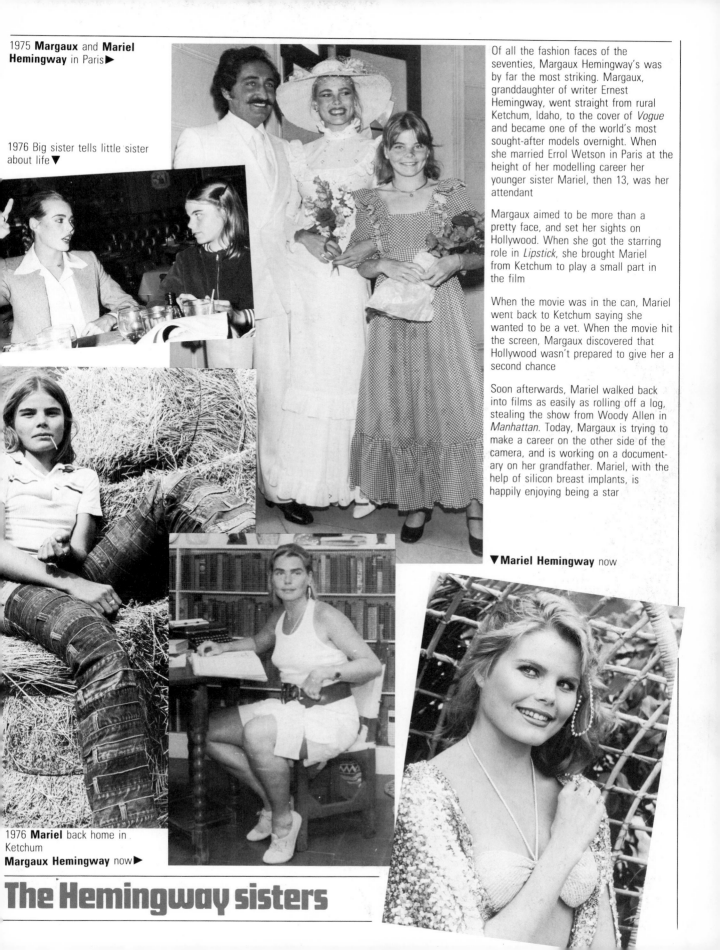

1975 **Margaux** and **Mariel Hemingway** in Paris ▶

1976 Big sister tells little sister about life ▼

1976 **Mariel** back home in Ketchum
Margaux Hemingway now ▶

Of all the fashion faces of the seventies, Margaux Hemingway's was by far the most striking. Margaux, granddaughter of writer Ernest Hemingway, went straight from rural Ketchum, Idaho, to the cover of *Vogue* and became one of the world's most sought-after models overnight. When she married Errol Wetson in Paris at the height of her modelling career her younger sister Mariel, then 13, was her attendant

Margaux aimed to be more than a pretty face, and set her sights on Hollywood. When she got the starring role in *Lipstick*, she brought Mariel from Ketchum to play a small part in the film

When the movie was in the can, Mariel went back to Ketchum saying she wanted to be a vet. When the movie hit the screen, Margaux discovered that Hollywood wasn't prepared to give her a second chance

Soon afterwards, Mariel walked back into films as easily as rolling off a log, stealing the show from Woody Allen in *Manhattan*. Today, Margaux is trying to make a career on the other side of the camera, and is working on a documentary on her grandfather. Mariel, with the help of silicon breast implants, is happily enjoying being a star

▼ **Mariel Hemingway** now

The Hemingway sisters

WHAT OUR ANIMALS SAY ABOUT US

Being blonde was all Brigitte Bardot and Doris Day had in common back in the fifties when they lit up movie screens around the world. As Miss Naughty and Miss Nice, they were as different as sugar and spice — one France's glamorous sex kitten, the other America's fresh-faced singing sweetheart. Since then, both have been badly disappointed by personal relationships, and today both lead reclusive lives — Doris Day in Beverly Hills with enough curs to fill a kennel, Brigitte Bardot in San Tropez with a menagerie that includes Jame, who was rescued from a vivisection centre in Marseilles. The men in their lives must have been pretty beastly to have driven them to the dogs this way

Brigitte Bardot (right) with Jame ● **Doris Day** (below) with one of her pets

Do we choose pets that look like we do? If Bo Derek (below) came back to earth as a dog, she'd probably be a sleek greyhound like her pet, Bolero. And another of her pet hounds bears more than a passing resemblance to her husband, John Derek

● **Bo** and Bolero

● **Bo** and her beau, husband **John**

Bo and her hound

Most members of the royal family dislike cats, but not Princess Michael of Kent, who goes her own way in this as in most things. Cats appeal to people with artistic and independent natures, Princess Michael to a T **Princess Michael of Kent** (below) with two of her eight Burmese cats

Sometimes we choose our pets for their character. Corgis are fiercely protective and intensely loyal — qualities that make them perfect pets for the Queen ● **The Queen** and her favourite corgi, Apollo

Witty Nigel Dempster, sharing his shoulder with the best friend England's leading social diarist could have — a little bird to tell him everything ● **Nigel Dempster** and feathered friend

A STYLE OF HER OWN

JUNE 1970

Margaret Thatcher, Conservative MP for Finchley North, London, age 44, with a university science degree and a spell at the Bar already behind her. Her style is fifties rather than seventies: her hairstyle is unflattering, her clothes unremarkable, and although she has handsome features, they have not been enhanced in any way. But she brightens herself up with her favourite pearls – a gift from her husband Denis

NOVEMBER 1973

Now Minister for Education and Science, Margaret Thatcher has a smarter look altogether. Her hair is longer and more stylish, and she has learned what an asset a good pair of earrings can be. But it is her clothes that are most interesting. In 1973, smart clothes for women consisted almost entirely of the over-cute little outfits that ladies of leisure wore to luncheon and bridge parties. For women over 30, the executive look did not then exist, so Margaret Thatcher's true sartorial style had for the moment to bide its time. Good Tory ladies still had to wear hats, so she did

MAY 1976

Now leader of the Conservative Party in Opposition, Margaret Thatcher has to lay her femininity aside in order to allay the fears of a party coming to terms with the first female political leader in modern British history. Fashion now provides executive looks off the peg for women, and she chooses clothes that are dark and plain, in order to minimize her femininity. She could have worn a tailored jacket with matching skirt, but it would have been wrong for her to look as though she were trying to be a man – being a woman is *quite* good enough. Her hair is high (to give her authority) and smooth, with no curls to suggest (however unthinkable) that there is any element of feminine flightiness. Gone are the little hats for ever. This is the look of a leader

JUNE 1978

On the brink of her successful election, Margaret Thatcher has her Party smoothly in control and can afford to assert her personal taste. Still high, her hair is now softer at the sides; her clothes are simple but no longer severe and the plain necklines have given way to flattering tie necks. She is about to break the mould of British politics for ever – and for the first time she is free to rise above the sartorial stereotypes of our age. From now on her style will be entirely her own – and her look is the look of success

MAY 1983

On the eve of the General Election that carried her into her second term of office, the Prime Minister is the picture of chic self-assurance, in full command of her capabilities and her style. While she has reverted to the dark colours of a leader at this testing time, she lets no one forget that the leader is a woman

APRIL 1984

Now in her second term of office, the Prime Minister has gone beyond being a mere national leader. She is an international statesperson, and plays a larger part on the world stage than any British Prime Minister since Harold Macmillan. She's never looked better – and neither have her favourite pearls. Power may corrupt men, but it suits this woman a treat

JUNE 1970

NOVEMBER 1973

MAY 1976

Margaret Thatcher

JUNE 1978

MAY 1983

APRIL 1984

IN THE SWIM

SPLASHING OUT · Swimsuits cut high on the hipbone are supposed to make your legs look longer. They do — but *only* if, like **Jerry Hall** (above), you've got the longest, straightest legs in Texas to start with

A BIGGER SPLASH · If you haven't, all a high-cut does is make your thighs look fatter. In a similar suit, **Linda Gray's** 35-inch hips look at least ten inches wider. So unless you like shooting from the hip, give this look a miss

WATCH THAT BAG!

Just because they're useful doesn't mean that bags are invisible – the right clothes and the wrong bag just don't mix

Bag of tricks

The Queen's classic handbags have been criticized for looking out of date, but there's more to them than meets the eye. Fashion harpies suggest that the Queen carry something light and modern like a pochette – but would we really like it if she did? On public occasions Her Majesty always looks poised and balanced, hands in the right place to wave, receive a bouquet or acknowledge an introduction. **Nancy Reagan**, clutching wildly, doesn't know what to do with her pochette or her hands. But that's the difference between being nouveau and being the real thing

Excess baggage

After taking a lot of trouble over their outfits, these two ladies have, to mix a metaphor, shot themselves in the foot. Both have gone for the bare look – **Pamela Bellwood** of *Dynasty* in a strapless dress and **Joan Van Ark** of *Knots Landing* in a one-shoulder dress – then ruined it by wearing a shoulder bag that puts a strap back just where it shouldn't be. No bag at all would have been better

Pamela Bellwood (right)

Joan Van Ark (far right)

Bags of style

Loretta Swit getting it white. Bags should always match or tone with the colour of the clothes you're wearing. If your dress has a very simple cut, it's nice if the bag is as pretty as this one, but if your dress is elaborate, keep the bag simple

The Queen Mother solving the problem of what to wear with a patterned fabric. A bag in the same fabric as your dress is the next best thing to invisible, and you'll never have to worry about it clashing with the rest of your accessories

Dyan Cannon getting it right. Glittery clothes call for glittery bags, and when you carry one it's best not to clutter yourself up with a lot of glittery jewellery

Morgan Fairchild (left) clutching a carpetbag that clashes with everything she's wearing ● Singer Bonnie Tyler (far left) sinking a light outfit with a heavy black shoulderbag

Ali McGraw (above) looking unsuitable. After going to the bother of getting a cape to match her suit, she's ruined everything with a dark bag and shoes ● Elizabeth Taylor (left) packing a squashy light bag that clashes with her cape ● Julie Walters (far left) making the biggest mistake of all. Whatever sort of bag you choose, make sure you keep it *closed*

Bad bags

SEEING DOUBLE ROYALLY

COAT IN THE ACT · **Viscount Linley** (below) and his sister **Lady Sarah Armstrong-Jones**, children of Princess Margaret and the Earl of Snowdon, wearing the same tweed coat. Sometimes he wears it, sometimes she wears it, and there shouldn't be any problem if they want to wear it together – this coat is bigger than both of them

ALL IN THE FAMILY · Not the same jacket, but definitely cut from the same kind of cloth. **Prince Andrew** (left) and his cousin **Viscount Linley** have a special reason for wearing this particular tweed – the pattern is called Prince of Wales check

FASHION KILLERS

UPPERS AND DOWNERS · **Tommy Tune** and **Twiggy**, each dressed in what the other should be wearing. A coat like his would make her look taller — a jacket like hers would take him down a peg. You can get away with dressing taller if you're tall, or shorter if you're short, but not if you go around with someone who's dressing in the opposite direction — then you just look like a very odd couple indeed. It's easier to change your clothes than your friends

TURBANDAGE · Turbans are meant to be worn high on the forehead. If you wear them low like **Barbra Streisand**, you look as though you're recovering from a head injury

CROWN TOPPER · **Prince Andrew's** hair is the real thing, but it looks just like a toupee here, and not a very good one at that. This must be the worst haircut in England. He shouldn't let his crimper put a crimp in his style this way

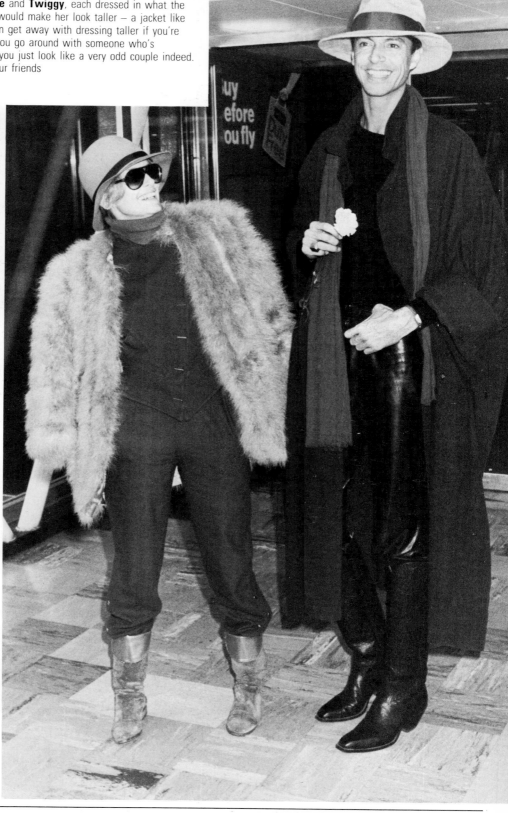

TWO DREADFUL · The moment every woman dreads — someone else, at the same party, in the same dress as you, looking better. It happened to top models **Cheryl Tiegs** and **Christie Brinkley** (right), but there was one consolation: they looked equally awful in their Fabrice-designed frocks

FOOT FAULT · **Barry Manilow** dealing his kilt a low blow with the wrong shoes

CLINGING TO THE WRECKAGE · Bodices ruched with elastic are supposed to give you a shape, but all they *do* give you is a sag. Wearing one, even thin **Nancy Reagan** looks like she's swallowed a salami sideways. This is not the way to look snappy

'EFFING AND BLINDING · Princess Michael of Kent thwarted by her hatbrim. What's the point of going to the Derby if you can't see what's going on? You can't look good if you can't take a good look

WHO'S WEARING WHOM · Great face, great figure, great legs — but all you notice is **Morgan Brittany's** eyecatching jacket. The worst thing you can do is let your clothes wear *you*

TRYING IT ON · No, they *aren't*. These two are winners of a French celebrity-lookalike contest. **She's** pretending to be the Queen, **he's** pretending to be Michael Jackson, and they're both making the biggest mistake of all. Wearing well means making the most of *yourself* — not trying to look like someone else

ACKNOWLEDGEMENTS

I would like to thank all those who have contributed to *The Way We Wear*: Paul Sidey of Hutchinson, Susan Hill, Linde Hardaker, Peter Hopkins, Catherine Mullen, John Austin, Ann Frost, Noel Rees, Ray Blumire of Alpha, Joanna Smith of Topham Picture Library, and Pushka.

Photocredits: abbreviations as follows: A = Alpha, P = Popperfoto, T = Topham Picture Library, RF = Rex Features, SI = Syndication International, CP = Camera Press, FS = Frank Spooner Pictures. *What Do We Wear Under What We Wear*: all by Alan Davidson; A. *Off the Shoulder*: Principal by Ron Gallela; A. Gray, Reagans; RF. Collins by Richard Young; RF. Seymour; SI. Princess of Wales; T. *Brooching the Subject*: Marilyn, Walters, Starr by Alan Davidson; A. Seymour, Princess Michael; SI. Culp by Jerry Watson; CP. Jackson; FS. *We Are What We Wear*: John in black and white tailcoat by Alan Davidson; A. All others T. *Prints*: Kent, Reagan, the Queen, Thatcher, Princess Anne; T. Harry, Collins by Alan Davidson; A. Princess of Wales by Jim Bennett; A. Queen Noor; A. Shields by Richard Young; RF. *The Big Dress*: the Queen, Reagan; P. Gabor; RF. Seymour; SI. Boyle by Alan Davidson; A. *Chopping and Changing*: Fawcett, Smith, Harry blonde, Taylor dark; RF. Harry dark; SI. Taylor light by Alan Davidson; A. *Faking It*: Princess Caroline, Tatler photograph by John Bishop; CP. Spencer; SI. Ford, Oxenburg by Alan Davidson; A. *Hanky Panky*; all T. *No One Can Look Good in Fur*: Gabor, Stewart by David Parker; A. Streisand, Ekland; SI. John, Hepburn; T. Loren; A. *You Can't Be Too Thin*: Mazel; SI. Reagan; RF. Welles by Alan Davidson; A. Weather Girls by David Parker; A. *Degeneration Gap*: Curtis by David Parker; A. Ekland; SI. *Getting It Off Your Chest*: Ono; RF. Taylor by Richard Young; RF. Newton-John by David Parker; A. Stark by Alan Davidson; A. Princess Michael; A. Hamnett; T. *Diana and Caroline*: jackets; A. Coats: Caroline; A. Diana; SI. Evening dresses: Caroline; FS. Diana; SI. Suits: Caroline; A. Diana; SI. *L for Leather*: Althorp by Alan Davidson; A. Kent, Fonda; T. Delon; A. Stewart, Collins; SI. *Growing Up*: Blair, Foster, O'Neal, Shields in 1978; RF. Shields now; A. *Messing About*: Reagan; RF. Ekland by David Parker; CP. Stark by Alan Davidson; A. Stewart by Richard Young; RF. Clark by Alan Davidson; CP. Taylor; FS. *You Can't Be Too Rich*: Onassis with Roussel; both A. All others RF. *Insight*: Hamilton; FS. King Carl Gustav, Maclaine; T. Perkins, Princess of Wales, Stewart; SI. Shields by David Parker; A. Loren; A. *Boy Oh Boy*: School, Black and Bleach Boys; A. All others RF. *Taking The Plunge*: Ample by Alan Davidson; A. Williams; A. Gabor, Gray, Evans, Streisand; RF. Stephenson, Helmond by Alan Davidson; A. Dickinson by Jerry Watson; CP. *Tiara Boom De Ay*: all T. *Two Weddings*: all T. *Boogie or Bogey*: Jackson 1977, 1981; RF. All others T. *Stars and Stripes*: Onassis, McCartney, Curtis, Minelli, Queen Noor; SI. Presley, Reagan, Hemingway, Tilton, Moore, Streisand, Bisset, Welch; RF. Ross by Richard Young; RF. Jagger, Connolly, Hockney, Carrera, Dylan, Jackson by Alan Davidson; A. Agutter, Harrison, Dunaway by David Parker; A. Beatty by David Parker; CP. Prince Andrew; T. Linley, Princess of Wales, Princess Anne by Jim Bennett; A. *Slimline Tonics*: Parton; T. Taylor, Roussos; RF. Slim Taylor, slim Roussos; A. *Unsuitable Suits*: John, Gill by David Parker; A. Ekland; SI. Stewart; T. *Coming a Cropper*: Streisand, Stephenson, Agutter; SI. Princess of Wales by Mike Lloyd; RF. *The Queen Mother*: all T. *Look Ear*: John; T. McGraw, Lauper, Mr T; RF. Princess Caroline, Maclaine, Ekland; CP. Princess Stephanie; FS. *Mum's the Word*: Curtis and Leigh, Shields, Bono, Landers, Tilton, Welch, Reagan; RF. Fisher and Reynolds; T. Grant and Cannon; A. Jackson by Alan Davidson; A. *Pearls of Wisdom*: Bacall, Gabor; RF. George, Miles by Alan Davidson; A. Hall by David Parker; A. Lumley; T. Henner by Jerry Watson; CP. *Diane Keaton*: all RF. *Over the Topping*: all T. *Belting Up*: Hack, Carrera, Evans, Jackie Collins, Lauper; RF. Rogers; CP. McGraw, Collins, Brittany, Bassey by David Parker; A. Williams, Oxenburg by Alan Davidson; A. Keaton; A. Andrews; T. Stewart; SI. *Hey Sister*: Collins; RF. Grimaldis in 1974; RF. Caroline at 16; CP. Stephanie at 16 by Lionel Cherruault; CP. Grimaldis now; T. Redgraves in 1967; T. Vanessa now; RF. Lynn now by Jerry Watson; CP. Hemingway; RF. *Animals*: Day, Bo with Bolero, Bo with hound, the Queen; SI. Bardot; A. Bo and John Derek; T. Dempster; RF. Princess Michael by Colin Shepherd; RF. *A Style of Her Own*: all T. *In the Swim*: Hall; SI. Gray by Roland Rentmeesters; CP. *Watch That Bag*: The Queen and Reagan, Cannon, Swit, Queen Mother by Alan Davidson; A. Bellwood, McGraw, Fairchild, RF. Walters by Richard Young; RF. Van Ark; A. Tyler by David Parker; A. Taylor; FS. *Seeing Double*: Linley, Linley, Prince Andrew by Alan Davidson; A. Lady Sarah by Lionel Cherruault; A. *Fashion Killers*: Brittany by Nils Jorgenson; RF. Streisand, Prince Andrew, Twiggy, Trying It On; T. Tiegs and Brinkley, Manilow; RF. Reagan; P. Princess Michael by Alan Davidson; A.